The SPORTS HEROES Library

Football's PUNISHING PASS RUSHERS

Nathan Aaseng

 Lerner Publications Company • Minneapolis

LIBRARY OF CONGRESS CATALOGING IN PUBLICATION DATA

Aaseng, Nathan.
    Football's punishing pass rushers.

    (The Sports heroes library)
    Summary: Outlines the careers of eight of the best pass
rushers in football. Included are Joe Klecko, Harvey
Martin, Fred Dean, Lee Roy Selmon, Big Hands Johnson,
Randy White, Art Still, and Bubba Baker.
    1. Football players—United States—Biography—
Juvenile literature. 2. Passing (Football)—Juvenile
literature. [1. Football players] I. Title. II. Series.
GV939.A1A167   1984   796.332'092'2 [B] [920]   83-17556
ISBN: 0-8225-1338-2

Manufactured in the United States of America

International Standard Book Number: 0-8225-1338-2
Library of Congress Catalog Card Number: 83-17556

1 2 3 4 5 6 7 8 9 10 93 92 91 90 89 87 86 85 84

Contents

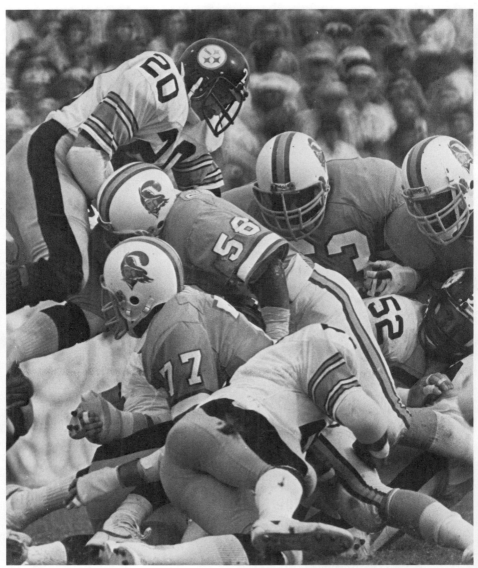

Even an All-Pro center like Mike Webster (52) can't dent the Tampa Bay defensive line. Here Dewey Selmon (58) and his brother Lee Roy (63) are about to tackle Pittsburgh's Rocky Bleier (20) for no gain.

Introduction

This book presents eight big reasons why the National Football League allows pass blockers to use their hands. The defensive linemen discussed are so huge, so powerful, and so fast that their opponents need all the help they can get to keep them away from the quarterback.

These defenders actually have several jobs to handle at their positions, but none is as important as rushing the passer. A strong pass rush is a defense's best weapon against the modern pro passing games. If an NFL quarterback is given time to throw, he can usually march his team downfield against the best pass defenders. But when the linemen come crashing in on him, he may be forced into rushing his throws. Some of these fall incomplete, and some can be intercepted. And every so often, a lineman charges in so quickly that he gets a defensive lineman's top thrill, a quarterback sack.

Cowboy tackle Randy White has broken through the blocking on his way to sacking the Colt quarterback.

A "sack" is not an official NFL term, but every football fan knows what it means. Anytime the quarterback is tackled while trying to throw, he is said to be sacked. The word first became popular in the 1960s. Great pass rushers had appeared on the scene, but no one kept track of any statistics for them. That is why there is no record of how many times Deacon Jones or Doug Atkins tackled the quarterback.

In the mid-1960s, the NFL began keeping track of how many times a *team* threw quarterbacks for losses. The Oakland Raiders recorded 69 sacks in 1967, the best total on record. The league has continued to ignore *individual* sacks as official statistics, but that has not kept football fans from paying close attention to this statistic.

More than one player is often in on a sack, so observers award a half sack to each player who helps out on a group sack and one point if he makes the tackle without help. Since people began keeping track, the best individual sack total for a season belongs to Coy Bacon. The veteran right end tallied 26 sacks while playing for the Cincinnati Bengals in 1976.

There are four methods that linemen can use to get through the wall of blockers protecting the quarterback. Joe Klecko often relies on his strength as he plows through blockers and drives them backwards. Randy White is a good example of a pass rusher who uses quickness. Although he weighs 270 pounds, he can outrun almost any quarterback in the league. Some, such as Bubba Baker, are masters at faking their blockers off balance. Finally, some rely on confusion. San Francisco has baffled opponents by switching top pass rusher Fred Dean from left end to linebacker to right end on different plays. Although each of the men in this book has special strengths, each uses a combination of the four methods to break through and pounce on the quarterback. Read on now and be thankful that these eight players aren't after you!

1
Joe
Klecko

For many years, quarterbacks looked forward to playing the New York Jets. The Jets' pass rush was so weak that passers felt cozy standing behind their pocket of blockers. They could pick out a receiver at their leisure without any Jet linemen getting close enough to even block their view. But all that has changed. Now the mere mention of the word "Jets" is enough to make quarterbacks scatter for cover.

The man most responsible for this turnaround is a truck driver named Joe. Joe Klecko was born in Chester, Pennsylvania, in 1953. The Kleckos were a family who believed in hard work. By the time Joe was 12, he was working full time in a gas station. Joe was not interested in books and never thought of going to college. Most of his spare time was spent in a garage, working under the hoods of cars.

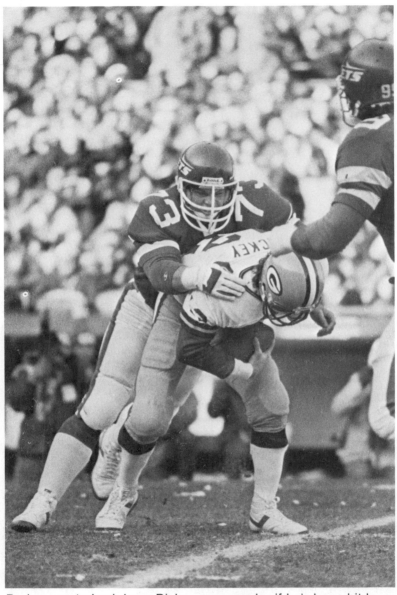

Packer quarterback Lynn Dickey may wonder if he's been hit by a truck, but it's only truck driver Joe Klecko!

10

Klecko was so interested in car engines that he did not bother to play football until his senior year at St. James High School. He was a large kid who had gone through his share of fights because of his baby-faced looks, so he caught on quickly to the fierce action of a football lineman. But when high school was over, Joe forgot about football and went back to his first love, trucks.

Joe was quite happy hauling his powerful rigs around until he found out about a local semi-pro league. Joe signed up with the league but took no money for playing to keep his standing as an amateur. And to be doubly safe, he played under an assumed name, "Jim Jones from the University of Poland." The play in this league often resembled a brawl more than an organized sport, but Joe was well able to take care of himself. He stood 6 feet, 3 inches and weighed about 265 pounds, and it seemed that most of that weight was packed onto a huge chest and shoulders. (Joe had also sported an impressive record of 34 wins in 35 fights as an amateur boxer.)

While playing in that league Klecko met the equipment manager at Temple University in Philadelphia. This manager alerted the school's coach, who somehow talked the reluctant Klecko into enrolling there. Although Temple was not a well-known football school, Joe did well enough there to win second-team mention on some All-American lists.

Klecko expected to cash in on his hard work at college by starting a career in the pros. But his hopes were jolted when he was not drafted by the Jets until the sixth round of the 1977 college player pool. A sixth-round draft pick normally has only a slim chance of making the team. Joe, however, earned a starting job in pre-season, and he even led his team in quarterback sacks during his rookie year. Klecko's raw strength helped him to lead the team in sacks again in 1978. It appeared that the Jets finally had the pass rusher they had been searching for.

But instead of leaving well enough alone, in 1979 the Jets tried an experiment. That year they moved Klecko to tackle and put young Marty Lyons in Joe's old position at end. The result was disaster. New York's pass rush was worse than ever, and the poor Jet defensive backs were picked apart by unhurried quarterbacks.

Klecko was switched back to end and Lyons to tackle when young Mark Gastineau was added to the lineup in 1980. After a year of learning to play

Top men in the New York Sack Exchange were the coldly efficient Klecko *(above)* and fiery Mark Gastineau *(below)*.

Joe's skill both at stopping the run, as he does here against the Giants, and at rushing the passer led many to call him the most valuable defensive player in football.

together, the young line suddenly surged through the opponents' pass blocking. Klecko's running form drew some snickers, but it was effective. Because he had so much muscle above the waist, Joe's legs seemed to be too small, and, when he charged ahead at full speed, he often looked as though he was falling over. But despite his style, he began to over-

14

power linemen at an incredible rate. During the first six games of the season, Joe forced 65 passes to be thrown quickly by panicky quarterbacks. He seemed to have worn a path to the backfield when playing the New England Patriots. In two games with the Patriots, Klecko pressured the quarterback 20 times.

While Klecko was doing the damage from his right end position, Gastineau was overwhelming foes on the left. The result was a fierce race for the pass-rushing lead between the teammates. Some teams felt as though they were caught in a vise between the hard-charging ends. Joe finally edged Gastineau, 20½ to 20, to top the league in sacks. With the ends leading the way, the Jets chased after the league record for sacks in a season. Nick-named the "New York Sack Exchange," Klecko, Gastineau, and teammates pinned quarterbacks behind the line 66 times. That was only one short of the league record held by the 1968 Oakland Raiders.

Klecko also proved he was more than just a pass rusher. He stood his ground against the run so well that he ranked second on the team in tackles. Some football writers were pointing to Joe as pro football's Player of the Year.

After sitting out most of the 1982 season with an injury, Klecko returned to join All-Pro Gastineau in chasing enemy quarterbacks.

It was New York's ferocious pass rush that gave the team its first shot at a play-off spot since the days of Joe Namath in the 1960s. The season came down to the final game against the Green Bay Packers. Both teams were fired up, knowing that they needed to win to keep their play-off hopes alive. From the very first series of plays, however, the Sack Exchange plunged the Packers into a deep depression. On almost every play, it seemed like a dam had burst in front of Packer quarterback Lynn Dickey. Klecko and his mates swarmed over Dickey throughout the entire game and recorded an astounding nine sacks! With that kind of showing from their defense, New York easily won the game, 28 to 3, and a play-off spot.

The following year, Klecko suffered a serious knee injury that put him out of the Jet lineup. But by the end of the season, he was already back in uniform. With Joe back in shape, that meant trouble for NFL quarterbacks, who could only hope that big trucker Klecko would move along down the road again soon. For as long as Joe remained interested in football, a lot of pro offenses were bound to stall!

At the moment, Redskin quarterback Billy Kilmer might find it hard to believe that Harvey Martin was once too scared to play football!

2
Harvey Martin

Harvey Martin's outgoing personality made him a favorite with the Dallas Cowboy fans. He was even given a spot on Dallas radio called "The Beautiful Harvey Martin Show." Actually, that title could have been used to describe almost any Dallas Cowboy game in 1977. The big Cowboy right end played a starring role in that championship season. And while Martin has done well throughout his career, that year he enjoyed the kind of season most players only dream about.

Not many who knew Martin in his early days would have guessed that he would be terrorizing pro football teams. Born in Dallas in 1950, Harvey seemed out of place in his fairly tough neighborhood. He was timid and afraid of other boys, and he did not want to get hurt playing football.

It wasn't that Harvey hated the game of football. No one in Dallas cheered harder for the young Cowboy football team in the 1960s. And no one suffered more when his favorite team was edged out for the championship by the Green Bay Packers two years in a row. But Harvey was content to watch the action, not become a part of it. Despite being larger than most others his age, Martin managed to avoid football until his junior year of high school. Even then it took a lot of peer pressure to get him to try it. His lack of enthusiasm on the field was almost embarrassing, and Martin was knocked on his back by players half his size.

Gradually, though, Martin learned to stand up for himself. By his senior year, he was using his size to play pretty tough football. He was not widely recruited by the colleges, but the coach at East Texas State University was excited by the progress Harvey had shown. He advised him to come to East Texas, where they were just getting a football program off the ground. That way Harvey would have time to learn his position without the pressure of a big-time winning program.

Martin agreed and attended the school, where he roomed with an upperclassman named Dwight White. White was a very aggressive defensive end

Harvey Martin

who went on to star in Pittsburgh's famous Steel Curtain defense. Harvey learned from White, and some of the older lineman's intensity crept into his play. By his senior year of college, Martin was one of the top players of the team that won a national title in its division in 1972.

Although East Texas was not known as a hotbed of pro prospects, the Dallas Cowboys had been closely watching Martin's progress. They liked his size—6 feet, 5 inches and 250 pounds—and his speed. With some improvement, they hoped the local boy would be a valuable addition to their defense. There was not much competition for Martin's services, so the Cowboys were able to wait until the third round of the 1973 draft before claiming him.

Being with the Cowboys helped Martin win some immediate notice. The successful Cowboys were often featured on national television, and a dozen or so times a game, an announcer would note that Harvey Martin was now in the game as a pass-rushing specialist. Martin relied mainly on his natural quickness to outrun tackles to the quarterback that year, and his nine sacks led the team.

The next season, Martin found good reason to get fired up. The Cowboys had brought in the first selection in the entire 1974 draft, defensive end Ed "Too Tall" Jones. Jones had huge athletic talent to go with his huge size of 6 feet, 9 inches and 260 pounds. Some were predicting the rookie would push Martin back to the bench, but Harvey rose to the challenge and attacked far more fiercely than he had his first year. He continued to be the Cowboys' best pass rusher, while Jones spent his first year as a reserve. When Too Tall finally moved into the lineup, it was at the other end position. With his right end job finally secure, Martin's outgoing personality started to come through. He won thousands of fans in Dallas and stepped in as the Cowboy

Although best known for his pass rushing, Martin is about to show the Broncos that he's no pushover on running plays, either.

leader when star defender Bob Lilly retired.

Then came 1977. Martin tore into his pass rushing that year, determined to be the best. In a defense perfectly suited to his skills, Martin was nearly unstoppable. Dallas liked to use a flex defense on the first two downs of a series. This was designed to stop running plays and often left opponents with a long ways to go on third down. Knowing that the other would have to pass to make the first down, Martin could then really turn loose his rush. He would crouch down like a sprinter settling into the starting blocks, his eyes big with anticipation.

One game Martin played against the St. Louis Cardinals that year especially stood out. Near the end of the half, the Cardinals were driving toward a score. Suddenly, the game was interrupted by "The Harvey Martin Show." He ran around, over, and through his opponent on four straight passing plays, and the Cardinal drive was shattered. St. Louis retreated to the locker room, shaken. By the end of the season, Harvey had rung up an incredible total of 23 sacks and 85 solo tackles. He was a popular choice as the NFL's Defensive Player of the Year.

Martin saved his finest performance of the entire season for Super Bowl XII. There the Cowboys faced the Denver Broncos and quarterback Craig Morton. Morton had thrown only eight interceptions all year. If given the time to throw, he could move the ball quickly against anyone. The Cowboys, though, were determined that Morton would not get the time. They turned loose their pass rush, and Morton must have felt as though the flood gates were opening on every play. Martin, Jones, and Randy White poured through the Denver line. The only passes Morton

The biggest suspense in Super Bowl XII was guessing who would win the race to the Bronco quarterback. On this play, Randy White won the right to squash Craig Morton by a step over Ed 'Too Tall'' Jones (72) and Martin (79).

could get off were desperate ones that resulted in four interceptions in the first half alone!

Any hopes the Broncos had of getting back into the game in the second half were erased by Martin. He broke through for two sacks, one of which caused a fumble. Along with teammate Randy White, he was awarded the game's Most Valuable Player Award for his efforts.

Along with co-Most Valuable Player, Randy White, Harvey makes his feelings known after Super Bowl XII.

Such a season was hard to match, and even Harvey has never been able to equal his success of that devastating season. But he has shaken off injuries to continue to be one of the league's most feared pass rushers. Just ask the Tampa Bay Buccaneers, who were overwhelmed by the Cowboy rush in a 38 to 0 play-off defeat in 1981. Or ask any of the eight quarterbacks he sacked in the shortened 1982 season, when he ranked fifth in the NFC in quarterback traps. They would be the first to admit that "The Harvey Martin Show" is in no danger of being cancelled.

With a swipe of his massive arm, Fred Dean proves to an ex-
teammate that the Chargers made a mistake in trading him.

3
Fred
Dean

You can't help but feel sorry for Fred Dean when you first see him line up at defensive end. Even at a quick glance, you can tell that he is the shortest and the smallest lineman on the field. It seems as if a linebacker has accidently wandered into the land of the giants. But it is a serious mistake to underestimate Dean. The San Diego Chargers did, and their fans may never forgive them. The San Francisco 49ers did not, and that bit of good sense may have won them a Super Bowl. You can be certain that no offensive tackle who wants to keep his job will ever treat Fred lightly again.

Fred was born in Arcadia, Louisiana, in 1952 and grew up on a small farm outside of Ruston, Lousiana. Like Harvey Martin, Dean considered himself a coward as a child. He had no confidence in himself and was so afraid of sounding ignorant that he almost never spoke. People misunderstood Fred and thought he was surly and mean.

Fortunately, Fred found an outlet for his frustration in football. Although he had never lifted weights, Dean was unusually strong from many years of hauling logs and baling hay on the farm. His strength drew some gasps from spectators during one of his high school games. On one play, Fred threw the rival quarterback so hard that the boy wound up under a fence outside the field.

Dean, who was called "Mean" Fred Dean after that play, went on to college at nearby Louisiana Tech. It was not a large school, but it had built a respectable reputation for football when Terry Bradshaw quarterbacked the team. Dean studied Shakespeare while at college and discovered some quotes that helped him gain confidence off the field. He still had all the confidence he needed *on* the field and was voted All-Conference each of his four seasons.

Despite Terry Bradshaw's success in the pros, scouts never knew what to expect from Louisiana Tech. It was difficult to get a clear picture of how good their players really were because their opposition was so weak. Although the San Diego Chargers

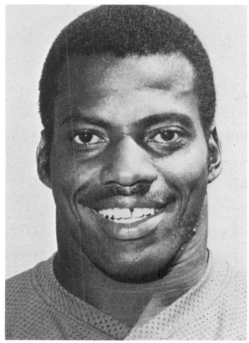

Fred Dean

knew that it was a gamble to draft Fred in the early
rounds, they still claimed him in round two of the
1975 draft.

Most experts took note of Dean's size and imme-
diately predicted that he would have to try out as a
linebacker. They were afraid that the 280-pound
tackles in the pros would trample the 6-foot, 2-inch,
228-pound rookie. But the Chargers soon found out
that Fred could hold his own against the burliest
opponents, and they found a place for him in their
rebuilt defensive line. From his first game as a pro,
Fred earned a starting position at right end.

It did not take long for rival tackles to discover that Fred was just about the fastest lineman on earth. He flew past blockers before they had a chance to straighten up. On end runs to the opposite side of the field, Fred chased and caught speedy running backs from behind. But what really took his rivals by surprise was his strength. Players who expected an easy time of manhandling the little end had all they could do to hold their ground against Fred's powerful charges.

A young Fred Dean shows Ram quarterback James Harris that, despite his size, he can't be brushed off.

Dean developed into the top pass rusher in one of the best pass-rushing units in the pros. Led by the charge of the line, the Chargers improved from one of the league's worst teams to one of its best. Despite a weakness at linebacker and a defensive backfield that was only average, the linemen kept the defense respectable. They especially hounded quarterbacks like Oakland's Ken Stabler and Pittsburgh's Terry Bradshaw who were used to fine pass protection.

Fred became a fixture in the Pro Bowl game, proof that the little lineman had made it big. The only ones who did not appreciate Fred were the people handing out paychecks in San Diego. After discovering that he was one of the lowest paid linemen in the league, Dean rebelled. He stayed out of training camp for awhile in 1980 and then again in 1981. The second time, he was determined to prove that he meant business and sat out the first five games of the year. Finally, the Chargers sent him to San Francisco for a second-round draft choice.

The 49ers were a young team that seemed improved over their 4-12 record of the previous year. They had beefed up their shabby defense by adding three prize rookies to the defensive backfield and by signing veteran Ram linebacker, Hacksaw Reynolds. This, plus their creative offense, had sparked

The 49ers' designated pass rusher has Green Bay quarterback Lynn Dickey right where he wants him.

the 49ers to a 3 and 2 mark by the time Dean joined them. The addition of a top-flight pass rusher was the final step that launched them toward the play-offs.

San Francisco used Dean intelligently. They liked to play a 3-4 defense in which the linemen were supposed to contain the blockers. Knowing that this style would not suit Fred, they kept him out of the starting lineup. But whenever the situation called for a pass rush, Dean went in as a fourth lineman. Whenever Dean entered the game, the other team's punting unit had to get ready to play. More often than not, Fred and his teammates would destroy the offensive play and force a punt. In a single game against the Rams, Fred sacked the quarterback four times and helped out on a fifth. Despite losing a good deal of playing time that season, Fred finished with 13 sacks. His pass rush was so impressive that, despite only playing part time, he was voted to the All-Pro team.

With Fred harassing the enemy quarterbacks, San Francisco won 10 of their next 11 games to earn a play-off spot. After beating New York and Dallas, the 49ers advanced to their first Super Bowl contest. There they put in a special formation to make use of Dean's talent. Leading the Cincinnati Bengals, 7 to 0, in the first half, they put Dean in as a roving middle linebacker. Dean blitzed from that position and helped force a sack to stop a Bengal drive. Switching back to defensive end, he continued to put on a fierce rush and the 49ers won, 26 to 21.

With a Super Bowl ring on his finger and All-Pro honors in his trophy case, Dean finds things are a little different now when he lines up for a play. No one feels sorry for poor little Fred anymore; instead the sympathy is with the unfortunate man who tries to block him!

4
Lee Roy
Selmon

Lucious and Jessie Selmon did not use tractors to farm their land outside of Eufala, Oklahoma; instead they used mules. Fortunately, they had plenty of available farmhands in the form of nine large, strong children. The youngest of the boys was Lee Roy, born in 1954. Like his brothers and sisters, he started working the fields at the age of five.

The Selmon farm produced a variety of crops, but the most famous thing grown there was football players. The three youngest boys formed a brick wall of defense that enabled the University of Oklahoma to reach the top of the college football ranks. And as good as Lucious, Jr., and Dewey were, it was Lee Roy who stood out as the top lineman in the entire country.

When facing Lee Roy Selmon, a quarterback often ends up with a poor view of the play!

Lee Roy's start in football was so embarrassing that he almost quit after his first day. Lucious, Jr., who was so strong he could throw a cow at age 11, tried the game first and encouraged his brothers to join. Dewey and Lee Roy, who also enjoyed rough play around the farm, went out for the junior high team together. (Although Dewey was the older by 11 months, the school cut-off date put them in the same class at school.) Both boys were rather pudgy, and the only uniforms that would fit them were a pair of enormous old ones. The pants kept slipping down during practice as the awkward brothers tried to run through the drills. It took a lot of talking to get Lee Roy back to the practice field after that!

The Selmons quickly developed into good athletes and starred at both football and basketball. They weighed nearly 230 pounds in high school and towered over their teammates. At first the football coach tried them in the offensive line, and then he came up with a wild plan. He put both Selmons in the backfield and dared the opposition to tackle them. Rival teams must have thought the world had been turned upside down when they faced a team with 140-pound blockers and 230-pound runners! But the strategy worked. Even with very little blocking, Lee Roy barged ahead for over

14 yards per carry in his senior year!

Lee Roy and Dewey then followed Lucious, Jr., to the University of Oklahoma. Lee Roy's days as a giant running back were over as the Sooners put him next to his brothers in the defensive line. It was a proud day for the Selmon family in 1973 when Oklahoma faced highly ranked Texas. For the first time, all three Selmons trotted out to take their positions in the starting lineup.

Texas was the first of many teams to discover that there was no way to get through the Selmon's "family gatherings" in the middle of the line. With Selmons swarming from all sides, life was miserable for opposing offenses. As they struggled off the field in defeat, they were said to have been "Selmon-ized." In the five years that Oklahoma started a Selmon in their line, they lost only three games.

By his senior year, Lee Roy was no longer just one of the boys; he had surpassed his brothers in fame. Pro scouts marveled over the fact that he was never knocked off his feet. At 6 feet, 3 inches and 255 pounds, he was also the largest of the family and just as fast as the others. In 1975 Lee Roy led Oklahoma to a national title and won the Outland Trophy as the country's top college lineman.

No one was surprised then when the Tampa Bay

Lee Roy *(left)* and Dewey *(right)* combined to lead the Buccaneer defense until Dewey was traded to San Francisco in 1982.

Buccaneers used the first choice of the entire 1976 draft to get Lee Roy. It was an unexpected bonus when the brand-new Bucs grabbed Dewey on the second round. But the thrill of playing together in the pros began to fade when the Selmons found out what it was like to play for a loser. During their first two seasons, the Buccaneers became a national joke as they lost 26 games in a row. Lee Roy was so embarrassed that he hated to leave the house even to get groceries after yet another Tampa Bay loss.

Four-time Pro Bowl star Selmon surges through to block a kick against the Packers.

No one was blaming Lee Roy for the Buccaneers' troubles, however. Even as opponents chuckled at Lee Roy's teammates, they treated him with respect. His combination of strength, moves, brains, and determination helped make the Bucs' defense surprisingly tough. Often they would shut down the opponent's offense only to lose when their own offense failed to move the ball.

Tampa Bay finally broke into the win column late in 1977, and they improved throughout the next season. There were some doubts, though, that Lee Roy would be able to enjoy some of this hard-earned success. Near the end of the 1978 season, he hurt his knee badly enough to need surgery. As with all serious injuries, there were fears that he would not fully recover.

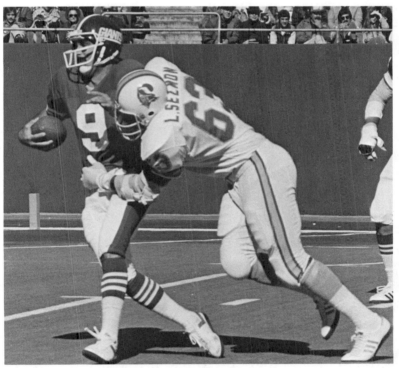

Plays such as this one against Giant quarterback Joe Pisarcik helped to make Lee Roy the Bucs' highest paid player.

The next season, the league found out that Selmon could still play. If anything, he was even better than before. Seldom has a defensive lineman played as well as Lee Roy did that year. Some coaches, noting how well the mild-mannered, gentlemanly Buc dominated the game, shuddered to think of the damage he could do if he ever got angry. Although opponents avoided his side of the field as if it were filled with land mines, Lee Roy still made 117 tackles. He played in a three-man line, where his job was mainly to contain blockers, and he still broke through for 11 sacks and forced quarterbacks to hurry their throws 60 times.

Lee Roy's performance powered the once laughable Bucs to the Central Division title of the NFC in 1979. In the play-offs, the Philadelphia Eagles learned that the Buccaneers were no laughing matter. Lee Roy seemed to have opened an express lane into the backfield from his right end position. Led by his charge, Tampa Bay stopped Ron Jaworski and Wilbert Montgomery and defeated the Eagles, 24 to 17. Then in the NFC championship game, the defense held the Los Angeles Rams to three field goals. Unfortunately, the Tampa Bay offense slipped back into their old habits and lost the game, 9 to 0.

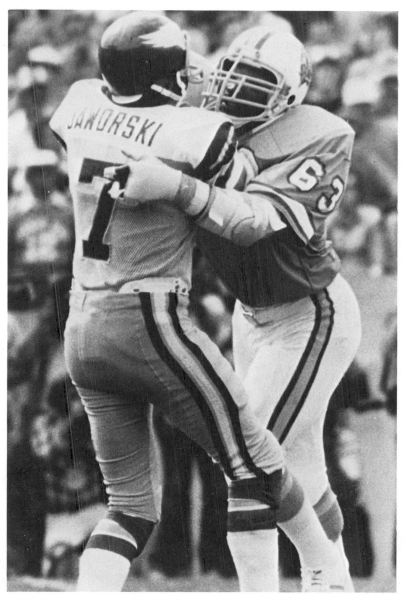

Philadelphia's Ron Jaworski couldn't shake loose from Selmon in the 1979 play-offs.

Minor injuries kept Lee Roy from top form during the next two seasons. But near the end of the 1981 season, he was showing his awesome skill again. In Tampa Bay's final game of the season, they faced the Detroit Lions for the division crown. As they held the lead and were driving for more points late in the game, Detroit seemed to have wrapped up the win. Suddenly, Selmon broke through to jar quarterback Eric Hipple into a fumble. Tampa Bay recovered and went on to score a late touchdown that gave them their second title in three years. Then in the Pro Bowl game, Lee Roy proved to be a true All-Star. Playing against the best blockers in the American Football Conference, Selmon broke through for four sacks. After yet another All-Pro season in 1982, it was obvious that Lee Roy's Selmonizing Service was back in operation!

5
Gary "Big Hands" Johnson

For most of his pro football career, Gary "Big Hands" Johnson has been just another tree in a tall forest. On one side of him in the San Diego Charger defensive line has been Fred Dean. Some have called Dean the best pure pass rusher in the game. All-Pro tackle Lou Kelcher lined up on Gary's left. The massive Kelcher was built like a refrigerator and was just as hard to move!

It was not easy to get much attention while squeezed between such company. So Big Hands had to be content with quietly running up the best pass-rushing totals of any NFL tackle in recent years. Not even the more famous Dean has been able to match Johnson's Charger records as a quarterback sacker.

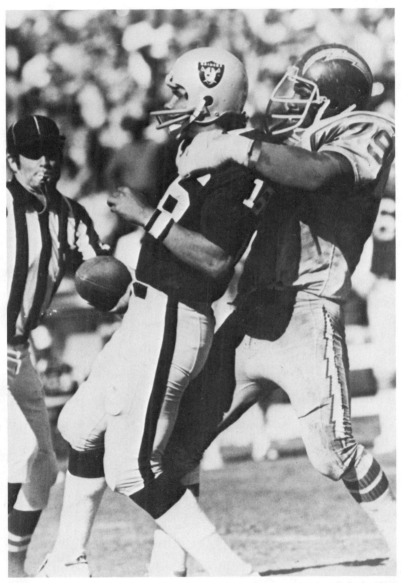

The new rule that calls a play dead when the quarterback is in the grasp of a defender saves Raider quarterback Jim Plunkett a rough trip to the ground at the hands of Big Hands Johnson.

Johnson was born in Shreveport, Louisiana, in 1952. He grew up in Bossier City, Louisiana, where he innocently gained a nickname that would go with him the rest of his life. While listening to a physical education teacher in the eighth grade, Johnson happened to grab a basketball. The teacher warned him to get his "big hands" off the ball. From that moment on, he was Big Hands Johnson.

Gary played football at Charlotte Mitchell High School and went on to college at Louisiana's Grambling State University. It was not only Gary's hands that were big. He stood 6 feet, 3 inches and weighed 245 pounds. Gary played four seasons at Grambling and won All-American honors during his senior year. Normally, a school as small as Grambling would not attract many pro scouts, but Grambling had a reputation for training players who had become pro stars. Gary was invited to compete in All-Star games at the end of the 1974 season. There he continued to uphold Grambling's reputation and was voted the outstanding lineman in both the Senior Bowl and the East-West Shrine game.

The San Diego Chargers desperately needed rebuilding when Gary was finished with college ball. During their past three years, they had won only 11 of 42 games. Using their high draft choices, the

Gary Johnson

Chargers looked to the Deep South for help in replacing their old defensive line. Big Hands was their first choice, and they went on to claim fellow Louisianan Fred Dean and Southern Methodist University's star tackle, Louie Kelcher.

Johnson did not crack into the starting lineup until midway through the season. Even then, it was an injury to starter John Teerlink that gave Gary the chance. He and his new linemates did nothing to change the Chargers' luck in 1975; the team won only 2 and lost 12. During Johnson's first two seasons, there was no sign that he could be an effec-

Lou Kelcher

tive pass rusher. During 1976 he hardly got close enough to a quarterback to know what one looked like. Despite starting in all 14 games that year, Big Hands contributed only 1½ sacks. Some wondered if the young Charger was too small to play tackle, the position of football's most enormous players.

But Big Hands learned to use his natural strength and quickness and showed rapid improvement. Suddenly he caught on to the tricks of pass rushing, and he sprinted past guards before they had time to straighten up from their stances. The Charger right tackle, who had reminded his teammates of a warm, gentle teddy bear, began to look much more fierce as he recorded 13½ sacks in 1978.

Meanwhile, the rest of the San Diego line had shown similar improvement. Although the Chargers were more famous for their high-powered offense, they also boasted the league's most terrifying rush. San Diego stormed past enemy lines for a league-leading 60 sacks in 1980. While Dean, Kelcher, and left end Leroy Jones had fine seasons, it was Johnson who led the charge. He set a San Diego record by trapping the quarterback 17½ times, a total which topped the entire AFC. That was awesome, considering that tackles rarely get as many sacks as the ends. (A defensive end usually has only one blocker to beat while the tackle often has to beat two.) NFL players named Johnson the Defensive Lineman of the Year. Many of his votes probably came from the Denver Broncos. In one game that season, Big Hands had personally wrecked the Bronco offense by throwing the quarterback for losses four times.

San Diego's weakness at linebacker and defensive back often erased much of Gary's work. Despite his great efforts in 1981, the Chargers often gave up points almost as fast as their famous offense could score them. Big Hands helped out on 106 tackles and led the team again in sacks with 10 to

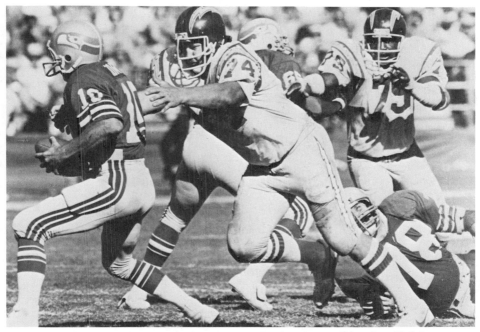

While Johnson was tied up by the Seahawks on this play, Kelcher wrapped up quarterback Jim Zorn.

keep the damage from becoming worse than it was. In the process, he set a Charger record with 60½ sacks in his career.

Johnson proved he could also put the squeeze on running backs as well as quarterbacks. In 1981 he forced two fumbles in San Diego's 22 to 20 win over Kansas City. Late in a game, he also pulled the ball loose from Detroit's Billy Sims to set up the Chargers' game-winning rally. Johnson showed he could do a little of everything that year by inter-

53

cepting a pass against Minnesota and scoring a touchdown on a lateral pass from Leroy Jones. Even though the San Diego defense around him performed terribly, Johnson's fine play earned him another Pro Bowl start.

When you consider how he treats offensive linemen, Johnson cannot really complain about being ignored. He does not bother to learn the names of all his opponents; uniform numbers and styles of play are all he needs to know about them. But if Johnson keeps up his All-Pro level of play, he will be meeting quarterbacks often enough to be on a first-name basis with them!

6
Randy
White

The Dallas Cowboys, with their computers and complex formations, have long been known as a thinking person's football team. But even the Cowboys sometimes outsmart themselves. That's what happened in 1975 when they tried to put the nation's top college lineman at linebacker. Fortunately, the Cowboys recognized their mistake in time to do something about it. After spending two years as a confused linebacker, Randy White instantly changed into the best defensive tackle in pro football.

Randy was born in 1953 and was raised near Wilmington, Delaware. He went through some tough times as a youngster when fights were almost a daily routine. But he was blessed with a strong body and grew even stronger with help from his job.

A lineman doesn't need a sack to be effective. Here White gets close enough to Bills' quarterback Gary Marangi to force a bad throw.

Randy lifted concrete blocks for his uncle and built up such strength that he was left alone.

Randy's father, a butcher, had played college football. At first he tried not to push his son into the game, but that gradually changed. When Randy attracted a baseball offer from the Philadelphia Phillies, his dad told him he would play college football instead. Randy had played on a losing football team in a weak conference in high school and had received few scholarship offers. His first choice of schools, the University of Delaware, did not offer four-year scholarships. Among the choices that were left, Randy's dad decided on Maryland.

Randy came to the University of Maryland weighing 212 pounds, which was fairly light for a linemen. He really had no choice but to play in the line because he was not fast enough to play anywhere else. While at school, White developed a liking for weight lifting. In fact, his coaches used to say that his address at college was: Randy White, Weight Room, University of Maryland.

Within a couple of years, White built himself up to 248 pounds, with tremendous strength in his upper body. Even with all that new bulk, he somehow actually improved his speed, too. Randy's time for the 40-yard dash dropped from an unimpressive 4.9 to an eye-catching 4.6. Maryland saw that all this power and speed was put to use on the football field. Randy terrorized opposing teams and helped Maryland to some of the finest years in its history. White was voted an All-American defensive lineman and even won the 1974 Outland Trophy as the country's top college lineman.

The Dallas Cowboys had been plotting for several years to get White on their team. They used trades to get the rights to the second player chosen in the 1975 college draft, and then they used that choice to draft Randy. The Cowboys knew just what they wanted to do with a man that fast and strong. They were going to put him in at middle linebacker to replace the aging Lee Roy Jordan. White was given the number 54 which had belonged to retired All-Pro Chuck Howley, and he was expected to produce like the old Cowboy stars.

Despite Randy's great athletic skill, he had trouble adjusting to the new position. One problem was getting used to the travel. Before he joined Dallas, Randy had never been far from home. The other problem was that middle linebacker is an especially difficult position for a newcomer. It takes a great deal of experience to be able to avoid blocks from all angles and to predict where a play is going.

Sometimes the only way to stop Randy is to hold him, as the Rams do here. (White hopes the officials are watching this illegal tactic.)

Randy looked forward to the times when he was allowed to play tackle in passing situations. He showed far more confidence at his old lineman spot and recorded seven sacks.

For two seasons, the Cowboys tried to groom White for the middle linebacker job. They finally gave up, and Randy was given a try at right defensive tackle, another spot with a great Cowboy tradition. Before retiring after the 1974 season, Bob Lilly had played that position so long and so well that he was known as Mr. Cowboy. But by the end of 1977, Randy's first year as a starter, he was putting on performances that even Lilly must have envied. He was voted to the Pro Bowl squad and topped off the year by making a complete wreck of the Denver Bronco offensive line in Super Bowl XII. White joined teammate Harvey Martin as co-winner of the game's Most Valuable Player Award.

Coach Tom Landry was not one to rave about his players, but it was hard to keep him quiet once he started talking about White. There were times when Randy would rush the passer and then wheel around and chase down the receiver 50 yards past the line of scrimmage. It didn't seem fair to opponents that a man who was widely known as the strongest Cowboy could also be one of the fastest.

It will take more than an arm to keep White away from Cardinal passer Jim Hart.

Ironically, Randy's reputation for speed and strength helped make certain he would never lead the league in quarterback sacks. Offenses spent most of their time preparing to play Dallas by deciding what to do about White. They have been willing to double-team and triple-team him, even though it has meant weakening themselves at other positions. Also, Randy's first task in the Cowboys' defense was to stop running plays rather than passing plays. Still Randy broke through for 16 sacks during 1978. At the same time, he fell only one short of leading his team in tackles, an amazing accomplishment for a lineman.

By the end of his second season at tackle, White had replaced such greats as Alan Page and Mean Joe Greene as the game's top tackle. United Press International (UPI) even voted him the league's top defensive player of that season.

Since then White's play has only gotten better. Some have said that he is not only the best tackle in football, he may be the best *player* in the game. But despite winning all of the honors a lineman can win, White still fears that when he takes the field for a game, he'll find he won't be good enough. When Coach Landry hinted that White's only possible weakness might be against the largest, strongest players, White worked out on weights with a fury. By the time training camp opened for 1982, White had packed on 20 more pounds of muscle without losing any speed.

Randy White

The fear of not being good enough has driven Randy White to play football as hard as anyone in the game. He seems to spend as much energy in a game as a man trying to build a house in one day. And if a player as skilled as White works that hard, think how hard the average blocker has to work to try and stop him!

63

The Raiders are known as football's most intimidating team, but big Art Still doesn't even flinch as the action heads his way.

7
Art
Still

At the University of Kentucky, Art Still majored in the scientific study of criminal behavior. If he had kept on with this career instead of turning to pro football, he could have been a walking advertisement for "the long arm of the law." Art is about as long, lean, and powerful as a person can get. Imagine a criminal's fright knowing that this 6-foot, 7-inch, 250-pound giant was hot on his trail!

That is a feeling that pro quarterbacks know all too well. Still has been handcuffing pro offenses ever since he entered the league. Although he is probably one of the least-known players in this book, many experts are convinced that he is close to becoming the very best at his position.

Arthur Barry Still was born in Camden, New Jersey, in 1955. He was one of 10 children in a family that was also large in build. The tall Still children were especially good at basketball, and several boys and girls in the family went on to star in the game at the college level.

Art certainly grew into an ideal height for the sport when he shot up to 6 feet, 7 inches. But he also had enough strength to enjoy playing in the defensive line in football. Oddly, Art went to play football at the University of Kentucky, a school more noted for basketball than football. During his four years as a starter, Still helped the Wildcat football team snatch some attention away from the basketball players. Art played well enough in his senior year to win unanimous All-Conference honors and lead Kentucky to a 10 and 1 record. But the college was serving a punishment for breaking National Collegiate Athletic Association rules and was not allowed in any post-season bowl games. Because of this, few fans heard of Art, even though he made many of the All-American teams.

The Kansas City Chiefs, however, had been doing their homework. Led by an enormous defensive line, the Chiefs had fielded a Super Bowl champion back in 1970. Players such as Buck Buchanon,

Still's height makes him appear as lean as a wide receiver in this pose for the University of Kentucky.

Aaron Brown, and Jerry Mays had allowed Kansas City to overpower their opponents. But those players were past their prime in the early 1970s, and the Chiefs had been stuck in a losing rut ever since. In 1978 they decided to go back to what had made them great before, and they sought a dominating defensive lineman. Still was their choice, and Kansas City made him the second player selected in the entire draft. Only Texas running back Earl Campbell was chosen ahead of him.

Art had played in a conference where most of the teams had run the ball, so in the pros it was easier for him to defend against the run than the pass. But he had shown signs of being able to break through for sacks, too. Although he weighed over 250 pounds, Still looked almost slim and was able to move quickly. He was so tall and fast and in such fine condition that, if given the slightest opening, he could blow past offensive tackles.

It took Art a while to learn the techniques of rushing the passer, and he collected only 6½ sacks during his first year. But even that was enough to lead the weak Chief rush. His play against the run, meanwhile, earned him All-Rookie team honors.

Art boosted his sack total to 8½ the next season, a respectable total when you consider the Chiefs' defensive situation. Kansas City had excellent defensive backs but poor linebackers, so most teams preferred to run against them. When opponents did pass, the Chiefs rushed only three linemen, which made sacks hard to come by. While Art had few chances to seek out the opposing passer, he saw plenty of running plays headed his way. Most of them went nowhere when aimed at his side of the line as he made 137 tackles! Two clubs in particular took a heavy pounding from the tall left

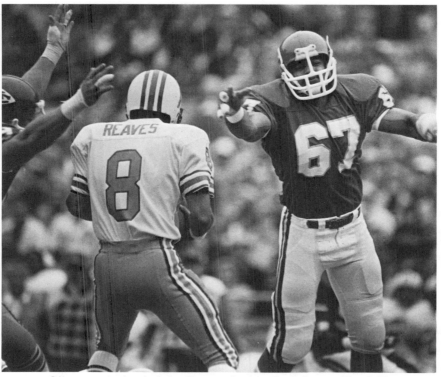
Oiler quarterback John Reaves learns that players like Still can get a pass rush with only a three-man line.

end. Art single-handedly stopped 15 plays in a game against the Pittsburgh Steelers. Then, on a rain-soaked field in Tampa Bay, he slogged through the puddles to make 20 tackles!

Kansas City improved each year, but not quite enough to challenge for a play-off spot. As a result, Art's performances were rarely seen by football fans outside of the Kansas City area, and not many

Still looks forward to the day when the Chiefs start winning so he can get a chance to play in the national spotlight.

people realized the outstanding defensive record that belonged to him in 1980. Despite the handicap of a three-man rush, Art got credit for 14½ sacks. That total, one of the best in the league, was more than anyone in the Chiefs' rich history of defensive linemen had managed. At the same time, Art made 140 tackles to rank second on his team. While fans scratched their heads and wondered who Art Still was, these statistics landed him on the All-Pro team.

Art injured his knee in a 1981 contest against San Diego and missed five games that season. That broke his record of starting in every game since joining the Chiefs. When he limped back into action, he continued to hold the line against running plays and to put pressure on quarterbacks. Still's solid play made the Chiefs one of the best teams in the league at defending against the run and put him in the Pro Bowl again in 1981 and 1982.

In 1981 Kansas City had enjoyed its first winning season since 1973. Although they faded badly the next season, most experts believed that the Chiefs weren't far from the play-off picture. With their line restocked with a huge All-Pro, the Chiefs only need some offensive punch to regain their past success. Cop. 2

Even a shifty runner like Green Bay's Terdell Middleton can't fake
out the acrobatic Bubba Baker.

72

8
Bubba Baker

How would you guess that Bubba Baker, the Detroit Lions' hulking defensive end, celebrated his first NFL quarterback sack? Perhaps with a victory dance? Some high-five hand slapping with a teammate? Did he swing his fist and jump high in the air or raise his arms and howl? No, Bubba Baker was so moved that he cried, and then he wandered offside on the next play.

It may not be the reaction you would expect from a man who slugs it out along the line where each play is a struggle to survive. But football is more than just a grim business to Baker. He approaches pass rushing as if each sack were a work of art. The linemen's pit is a dance floor to him. Baker has found more ways to whirl past an offensive tackle than any other man in the game.

James Albert London Baker was born in sunny Jacksonville, Florida, in 1956. The climate in Newark, New Jersey, where he grew up was not nearly so cozy. Baker lived in a rough neighborhood and saw riots and shootings on the streets before he had even entered grade school. His dad had died when Bubba was six, and that left his mother to raise her children alone. She was scared into being tough, almost mean, to Bubba. He later said that, compared to his mom, even the harshest football coach seemed gentle.

Baker managed to stay out of trouble, and he used sports as an outlet for his energy. He had to look hard, though, to find places to play his games as the only place near his neighborhood with enough grass for a football game was a cemetery.

"Bubba" Baker attended Weequahlic High School, where he starred as a basketball player. His nickname did not come from being compared to the powerful football star, Bubba Smith. It was a shortened form of his first nickname, "Bubbles," which described his outgoing personality. His main role on the team was as a rebounder, and few high school players dared to challenge big Bubba for rebounds. Baker helped clear the backboards for a team that won four straight state championships.

Al "Bubba" Baker

Bubba's basketball skills earned him a scholarship to Colorado State University. There he continued to throw around his 6 feet, 6 inches and 240 pounds and was truly a fierce rebounder. He used his strength a little too much, though, according to college referees. After being in foul trouble constantly on the court, he decided to move to a sport where he could use his strength more freely. Instead of using football moves on the basketball court, Baker began to use his basketball moves on the football field.

Bubba was a creative person who chose art as his area of study. Rather than try to overpower opponents, he used his creativity on the football field, too, to experiment with all kinds of fakes and moves. He developed his own style of pass rushing and resembled a basketball forward driving down the lane as he faked out his opponents. Although he did not start playing regularly until his junior year, Bubba became one of the top college pass rushers.

The Detroit Lions drafted Baker in the second round in 1978. Eight teams selected college linemen ahead of Baker. But by the end of the year, almost all of them wished they had chosen Bubba. His head fakes, spins, and twirls pumped new life into the Lions' pass rush. Fans called the Detroit front four "The Silver Rush," named after the Silverdome where they played. Bubba was the lineman who struck the jackpot most often as he recorded 23 sacks to lead the entire NFL. Even in the heat of the action, his old nickname of Bubbles still fit his personality. He treated the field as if it were a disco floor and could hardly stand still between plays. He was a man who was truly happy in his work, and he sang and laughed while on the field. His opponents, however, were rarely in a good mood when facing him. Despite being hit with

Baker's rush is so fierce that most teams have to double-team him. Here the Browns use tight end Ozzie Newsome (82) to help out their left tackle.

tougher blocking strategies, Bubba still managed 16 sacks in his second year. That total would have set a team record for many pro teams, but Baker apologized for having an off year.

In 1980 Bubba sat out for a while in a contract dispute and got off to a slow start. But the pass-rushing artist finished strong and wound up with

18 quarterback traps. The next year, he was bothered by injuries. He missed five games and was not in top form for others, but he still collected 10 sacks. Baker broke through for a club-leading 8½ sacks in 1982 to give him a total 75½ sacks in his 67 games, by far the most of any lineman in football. Baker did not need to get his hands on the quarterback to help the Lion rush, either. As opponents put more effort into blocking Baker, the rest of the Lions started to pour through offensive lines. With Bubba tying up several opposing blockers, the Lions led or tied the NFC record in sacks in both 1981 and 1982.

Bubba's pass rush was so good that many believed he was only a pass-rushing specialist. Rumors spread that the way to beat the Lions was to run at Baker. But while Bubba was not quite as creative on running plays as he was on the rush, he was nearly as effective. He showed he was no patsy against the run when he helped Detroit finish first in the conference in defending against the run in 1980, 1981, and 1982.

Another contract disagreement led the Lions to trade their star in the 1983 pre-season. The St. Louis Cardinals welcomed him and hoped he would join young Curtis Greer in giving them the outside pass rush they had lacked for years. They

New Cardinal Baker lets Green Bay's David Whitehurst know that the knockdown was nothing personal—just a part of his job.

were counting on Bubba to keep searching for new moves to try on unsuspecting offensive tackles. They knew he took such pride in his pass-rushing skill that he would not rest on the praise he had received from his previous work. Instead the sack artist would want to make sure his work remained on display for fans all over the country.

ACKNOWLEDGMENTS: The photographs are reproduced through the courtesy of: pp. 4, 38, 41, 42, 43, 45, Tampa Bay Buccaneers; pp. 6, 18, 21, 23, 56, 59, 61, 63, Dallas Cowboys; pp. 10, 25, 26, 34, 72, 79, Vernon J. Biever; pp. 13, 14, 16, New York Jets Football Club, Inc.; pp. 28, 31, San Francisco 49ers; pp. 32, 48, 50, 51, 53, San Diego Chargers Football Club; pp. 64, 69, 70, Hank Young Photography; p. 67, University of Kentucky Athletics Association; pp. 75, 77 (George Gellatly), Detroit Lions. Cover photograph courtesy of New York Jets Football Club, Inc.